Clark's Horn

by Carlos Ash
illustrated by David Austin Clar

Practice Decodable 38

McGraw Hill Education

Bothell, WA • Chicago, IL • Columbus, OH • New York, NY

MHEonline.com

Send all inquiries to:
McGraw-Hill Education
8787 Orion Place
Columbus, OH 43240

ISBN: 978-0-02-133154-3
MHID: 0-02-133154-5

Printed in the United States of America.

7 8 9 CTM 23

Clark is in a band.

He has a horn.

Clark's band marches at parks.

Clark has his hat and little scarf.

Clark has marks on his arms.

"I look sharp!" said Clark.

Clark started to jump in his car.
Then he stopped.

"I left the horn!" he grinned.
"That is not smart!"